BESTIARY I BESTIARIO

BESTIARY / BESTIARIO

a poem by

PABLO NERUDA

translated by ELSA NEUBERGER

with woodcuts by

ANTONIO FRASCONI

A Harvest Special

Harcourt Brace Jovanovich
New York and London

Printed in the United States of America

The text was originally published as "Bestiario" in *Estravagario*, a collection of poems
by Pablo Neruda, published by Editorial Losada, S.A., Buenos Aires.

Library of Congress Cataloging in Publication Data
    Neruda, Pablo, 1904–1973.
      Bestiary. Bestiario: a poem.
      (A Harvest special HB 292)
      English and Spanish.
        I. Frasconi, Antonio, illus. II. Title.
     III. Title: Bestiario.
     [PQ8097.N4B4 1974]   861   74–6154
      ISBN 0–15–611860–2

First Harvest edition 1974
  B C D E F G H I J

PABLO NERUDA reminds one of another Pablo, Pablo Picasso, and not merely because both are Pablos, for, after all, Neruda's given name is Neftalí Ricardo Reyes. Their resemblance goes much deeper: it has to do with their fertile, chameleon-like creativeness, their constant, unpredictable transformations, and, of course, their world outlook. Both are inextricably bound to the Hispanic tradition, yet both have transcended it without totally shedding its most precious essences. Often their arts have been bafflingly esoteric, mysteriously hermetic — witness Neruda's middle period, with the luxuriantly baroque *Residence on Earth*. Yet at the moment of urgent social commitment — at the explosion and bloody mess of the Spanish Civil War — his register changed, the Gongorist afflatus was muffled, and his utterance became pristine clear. This directness characterized *Spain in the Heart*. Eventually the two voices — the highly aesthetic and the burning socially conscious — mingled in the symphonic *Summits of Macchu Picchu*, one of his most notable achievements.

The exciting *Bestiary* now at hand, and so enhanced by Frasconi's superb woodcuts, mirrors an omnipresent concern of Neruda: his love for and understanding of Nature. From his earliest writings, the geology and geography, the fauna and flora of Chile emerged in lyrical splendor and thereafter in *Residence on Earth* (the title is significant) he highlighted, in changing colors and sounds, the wind and the rain, the sea, rocks, and plants, the buoys, the distant whistles, the tolling of bells. In recent years Neruda intimately communed with the most elementary aspects of life, as his *Odas elementales* so eloquently show in all their stark simplicity. With *Bestiary*, unabashed, with his characteristic and very contagious enthusiasm, Neruda endeavors to establish contact with the animal world. The bestiaries, which delighted and instructed prescientific medieval readers, attain in Neruda's *Bestiary* an original form, humorous, warm, and obliquely satirical. The world of "shrewd capitalists" and "systematic women" appears insipid and colorless when faced by the sweet, sonorous husky-voiced frogs, the star-weaving spiders, the genital-eared rabbits, and the sanskrit fleas. After Neruda's *Bestiary* one will never stop wondering what was the name of that cat. . .
ANGEL FLORES

If I could speak with birds,
with oysters and with little lizards,
with the foxes of the Dark Forest,
with the exemplary penguins;
if the sheep,
the languid woolly lap dogs,
the cart horses would understand me
if I could discuss things with cats,
if hens would listen to me!

Si yo pudiera hablar con pájaros,
con ostras y con lagartijas,
con los zorros de Selva Oscura,
con los ejemplares pingüinos,
si me entendieran las ovejas,
los lánguidos perros lanudos,
los caballos de carretela,
si discutiera con los gatos,
si me escucharan las gallinas!

It has never occurred to me to speak
with elegant animals:
I am not curious
about the opinion of wasps
or of racing mares.
Let them settle matters while flying,
let them win decorations by running!
I want to speak with flies,
with the bitch that has recently littered,
and to converse with snakes.

Nunca se me ha ocurrido hablar
con animales elegantes:
no tengo curiosidad
por la opinión de las avispas,
ni de las yeguas de carrera:
que se las arreglen volando,
que ganen vestidos corriendo!
Yo quiero hablar con las moscas,
con la perra recién parida
y conversar con las serpientes.

When I had feet for walking
in triple nights now past,
I followed the nocturnal dogs,
those squalid travelers
that trot in silence
with great haste traveling nowhere,
and I followed them for many hours.
They mistrusted me,
ah, poor stupid dogs,
they lost their opportunity
to pour out their sorrows,
to run through streets of ghosts
with grief and tail.

Cuando tuve pies para andar
en noches triples, ya pasadas,
seguí a los perros nocturnos,
esos escuálidos viajeros
que trotan viajando en silencio
con gran prisa a ninguna parte
y los seguí por muchas horas,
ellos desconfiaban de mí,
ay, pobres perros insensatos,
perdieron la oportunidad
de narrar sus melancolías,
de correr con pena y con cola
por las calles de los fantasmas.

I have always been curious
about the erotic rabbit.
Who excites them and whispers
in their genital ears?
They procreate endlessly
and pay no attention to Saint Francis,
they hear no nonsense:
the rabbit mounts and remounts
with an inexhaustible organism.
I wish to speak with the rabbit,
I like his flighty habits.

Siempre tuve curiosidad
por el erótico conejo:
quiénes lo incitan y susurran
en sus genitales orejas?
Él va sin cesar procreando
y no hace caso a San Francisco,
no oye ninguna tontería:
el conejo monta y remonta
con organismo inagotable.
Yo quiero hablar con el conejo,
amo sus costumbres traviesas.

Spiders are wasted
on exasperating naturalists who
in their foolish pages
see them with a fly's eyes,
describe them as devouring,
carnal, unfaithful, sexual, lascivious.
For me this reputation
provides a portrait of those who
impute it to them:
the spider is an engineer,
a divine watchmaker,
that the idiots detest
for a fly more or less.
I want to converse with a spider:
I want her to weave me a star.

Las arañas están gastadas
por páginas bobaliconas
de simplistas exasperantes
que las ven con ojos de mosca,
que la describen devoradora,
carnal, infiel, sexual, lasciva.
Para mí esta reputación
retrata a los reputadores:
la araña es una ingeniera,
una divina relojera,
por una mosca más o menos
que la detesten los idiotas,
yo quiero conversar con la araña:
quiero que me teja una estrella.

Fleas interest me so much
that I let them bite me for hours.
They are perfect, ancient, Sanskrit,
machines that admit of no appeal.
They do not bite to eat,
they bite only to jump;
they are the dancers of the celestial sphere,
delicate acrobats
in the softest and most profound circus;
let them gallop on my skin,
divulge their emotions,
amuse themselves with my blood,
but someone should introduce them to me.
I want to know them closely,
I want to know what to rely on.

Me interesan tanto las pulgas
que me dejo picar por horas,
son perfectas, antiguas, sánscritas,
son máquinas inapelables.
No pican para comer,
sólo pican para saltar,
son las saltarinas del orbe,
las delicadas, las acróbatas
del circo más suave y profundo:
que galopen sobre mi piel,
que divulguen sus emociones,
que se entretengan con mi sangre,
pero que alguien me las presente,
quiero conocerlas de cerca,
quiero saber a qué atenerme.

I have never been able to become
intimate with ruminants in any deep way,
yet I am a ruminant;
I do not understand their not understanding me.
I must take up this subject
grazing with cows and oxen,
and working out plans with bulls.
In some manner I will know
so many intestinal things
which were hidden within
like clandestine passions.

Con los rumiantes no he podido
intimar en forma profunda:
sin embargo soy un rumiante,
no comprendo que no me entiendan.
Tengo que tratar este tema
pastando con vacas y bueyes,
planificando con los toros.
De alguna manera sabré
tantas cosas intestinales
que están escondidas adentro
como pasiones clandestinas.

What does the pig think of the dawn?
They do not sing but they hold it up
with their great rosy bodies,
with their hard little feet.

Qué piensa el cerdo de la aurora?
No cantan pero la sostienen
con sus grandes cuerpos rosados,
con sus pequeñas patas duras.

The pigs hold up the dawn.

Los cerdos sostienen la aurora.

The birds consume the night.

Los pájaros se comen la noche.

And in the morning the world is deserted:
the spiders, men, dogs, the wind sleep,
pigs grunt and day breaks.

Y en la mañana está desierto
el mundo: duermen las arañas,
los hombres, los perros, el viento,
los cerdos gruñen, y amanece.

I want to speak with pigs.

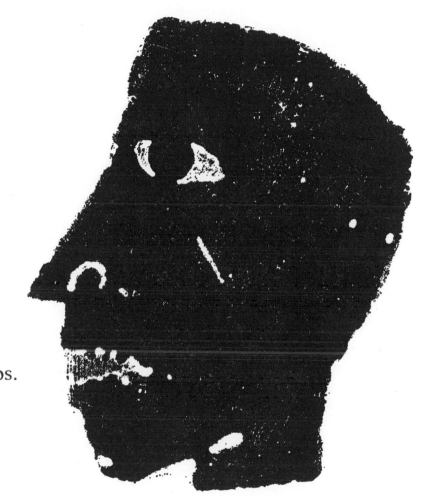

Quiero conversar con los cerdos.

Sweet, sonorous, husky-voiced frogs!
I always wanted to be a frog for a day,
always loved the pool, the leaves
fine as filaments,
the green world of the watercress
where the frogs are masters of the sky.

Dulces, sonoras, roncas ranas,
siempre quise ser rana un día,
siempre amé la charca, las hojas
delgadas como filamentos,
el mundo verde de los berros
con las ranas dueñas del cielo.

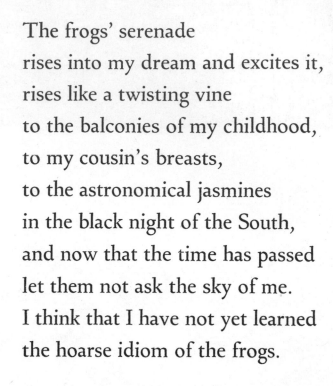

The frogs' serenade
rises into my dream and excites it,
rises like a twisting vine
to the balconies of my childhood,
to my cousin's breasts,
to the astronomical jasmines
in the black night of the South,
and now that the time has passed
let them not ask the sky of me.
I think that I have not yet learned
the hoarse idiom of the frogs.

La serenata de la rana
sube en mi sueño y lo estimula,
sube como una enredadera
a los balcones de mi infancia,
a los pezones de mi prima,
a los jazmines astronómicos
de la negra noche del Sur,
y ahora que ha pasado el tiempo
no me pregunten por el cielo:
pienso que no he aprendido aún
el ronco idioma de las ranas.

If this is so, how am I a poet?
What do I know of the multiplied
geography of the night?

In this world which runs and is silent,
I want more communications,
other languages, other signs,
I want to know this world.

Si es así, cómo soy poeta?
Qué sé yo de la geografía
multiplicada de la noche?

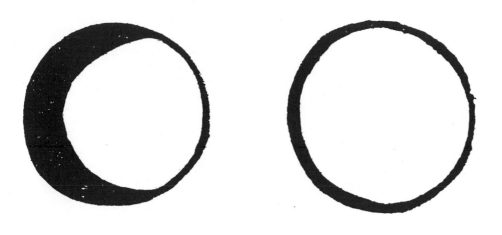

En este mundo que corre y calla
quiero más comunicaciones,
otros lenguajes, otros signos,
quiero conocer este mundo.

Everyone has been contented
with the sinister presentations
of shrewd capitalists
and systematic women.
I want to speak with many things
and I will not leave this planet
without knowing what I came to seek,
without investigating this matter,
and people do not suffice for me,
I have to go much further
and I have to go much closer.

Todos se han quedado contentos
con presentaciones siniestras
de rápidos capitalistas
y sistemáticas mujeres.
Yo quiero hablar con muchas cosas
y no me iré de este planeta
sin saber qué vine a buscar,
sin averiguar este asunto,
y no me bastan las personas,
yo tengo que ir mucho más lejos
y tengo que ir mucho más cerca.

Therefore, gentlemen, I am going
to converse with a horse.
May the poetess excuse me,
and the professor forgive me.
My whole week is taken up,
I have to listen to a confusion of talk.

Por eso, señores, me voy
a conversar con un caballo,
que me excuse la poetisa
y que el profesor me perdone,
tengo la semana ocupada,
tengo que oír a borbotones.

What was the name of that cat?

Cómo se llamaba aquel gato?